THE
Ballad OF Values
AT CLOSE RANGE

VOLUME 1
POETRY LYRICS

STANLEY LYTE

authorHOUSE®

AuthorHouse™
1663 Liberty Drive
Bloomington, IN 47403
www.authorhouse.com
Phone: 833-262-8899

Published by AuthorHouse 11/21/2023

ISBN: 979-8-8230-1695-7 (sc)
ISBN: 979-8-8230-1694-0 (e)

Library of Congress Control Number: 2023920730

CONTENTS

EPISODE 1

BREATHS DRAWN EASILY
AS BOTH OF US WANDER

Both of us wandered around urban park,

And looked up beyond the clouds staring

Shortly after time, the sun began to set

As' emerged countless visible stars

"far off in space to our bare eyes"

Joyfully, both of us searched for cardinal point
Tropic of Capricorn

Hurriedly, on winter solstice watching

A "phenomenal sight" as spectators

Breaths Drawn Easily As Both Of Us Wander

Watching the sun's radiance coming out of northern hemisphere!

Brilliant rays cast a shadow on a sundial!

Fore, sharing clock calendar hours

While, adjusting telescope from sunshine's glare

"confounded our eyesight range"

As' we tried to gaze afar,

And overexcited as usual

Both of us find new adventure, planning journey for another time

Breaths Drawn Easily As Both Of Us Wander

Both of us on one similar afternoon, within seconds

As' expected rises vapors with a aroma

"familiar like a wholesome bunch of apricots"

A scented savory sweetness!

Faintly, wispy sensations made our spirit content

"spending hours walking in green fields!"

Finally, both of us stood still,

And earth's biosphere freshens our bodies

Breaths Drawn Easily As Both Of Us Wander

Outdoors a wind stream overcame both of us

As' warm soothing breaths inhaled

While, finding both our lives worthy

Fore, vigilant again, both of us then exhaled!

Breaths Drawn Easily As Both Of Us Wander

EPISODE 2

✦✦✦

IN FAITH PRAYING TO LORD
OF LORDS TO BE SAVED

I recall my good lord for covenant

Whom has a chosen nation

Easily, always certain of my righteous guide

While, living for redemption to be uplifted, in the
good lord's holy land,

And my soul abide by tabernacle's law

Fore, offering devotions to faithful imminent son

Firmly, on right side of heavenly station

Oh' Thou merciful son of the most high

5

In Faith Praying To Lord Of Lords

Above his heavenly eminence, our good lord resides

"praised by worshipers throughout countries"

A luminous priestly corridor

Fore, pathway to a promised paradise

While, forever forever evermore praises!

Loudly, proclaiming, the word of my good lord

Fore, my patience is fine

Hourly, standing by until my good lord arrive to make a judgment

In Faith Praying To Lord Of Lords

On a forthcoming day

Overly, I will embrace my faith

Righteously, in the good shepherd

Whom, taught worthwhile lessons for us to follow

While, revealing his Father's most high nature!

Fore, those living by the Ten Commandments should have salvation,

And believe, the name of his son

Freely, praising lord god with their hearts

In Faith Praying To Lord Of Lords

Great is our lord work

Fore, preparing a place to walk

Faithfully, with grace in Jesus name

Fore, his spirit can be poured upon us

In Faith Praying To Lord Of Lords

EPISODE 3

⚜

COMPLIMENTS TO PERFORMERS

Every lived moment, I have a soul

Generally is of true value

Consciously, drawn inside a lighted tunnel

Fore, leading to this occasion for leisure

Musically, reveals shows of melodrama

Comfortable, to find motivated my choice!

While, watching a conductor with a symphony

"playing musical's finest notes"

Compliments To Performers

Swiftly, I applaud to give musicians confidence

Loudly, cheering to show my favor

"standing over chair, simply to boost their ego!"

While, Focusing on the baton's movement

Whom lead conducts musicians to play,

And sing musical notes in unity

"sentimental soothing lyrics of sentiment"

Worldly, sent to every listener everywhere!

Compliments To Performers

A lasting moment at show

Awesomely, escalates concerto as time lapses

Slowly, on a wristwatch to keep the audience's attention, on live performers

While, myself with others watching from our seats

As' musicians play musical notes of sincerity

Gladly, sent a soothing sensation
through my body

"transferring my senses to another mellow place"

Soundly, a familiar welcoming call

Compliments To Performers

Aloud, I applauded insanely into a spectacle of myself

Excitedly, right in front of audience clapping

"afterwards excitement has exhausted me"

Nearly, to a point of being worn out at a vibrant moment

Outwardly, heard soothing musical tones

"steadfast was making my eardrums restless"

Foremost, show inside the Auditorium,

And I took a couple of minutes from a show that is sensational to pause

Compliments To Performers

I allow myself some rest

Usually, to feel like my self again

Mostly, waiting for favorite in-row

Choral symphony, to begin their performance

Compliments To Performers

EPISODE 4

A HEARTFELT SUM
WARMS UP US

Adoring a lovely moment

Vainly, is sort of a quest

Fore, both of us plainly

About, social relationship, having to bring upfront

"reading the first page of a open book"

While, leaving both of us trying to figure out how this story will end

Only, noting both of us are sharing personal information in a therapy session!

As' curiosity rests lightly on our minds

A Heartfelt Sum Warms Up Us

Touching base at an unfortunate moment is unwanted,

And Vows made aloud kept on record

"found at municipal building recalls"

While, unforeseen rising emotions has taken control!

Wherefore, following crucial seconds, staying balanced, to regain a route

Literally, answering unsolved emotions, around both of us

As' needle always points north south on a compass

Wisely, brings both of us to end of search

A Heartfelt Sum Warms Up Us

Supposedly, infatuation is the reason

Fore, fallen in love quicker than a fool,

And both of us were liable at a point

"unmovable, since first date clearly!"

As' an open gate in heaven

Both of us were aware of love

"both of us had a chance to hide feelings!"

Fore, both of us said in our heart being happy is a worthwhile moment

A Heartfelt Sum Warms Up Us

Matched with right soulmate,

And nothing else can compare

As' both our emotions let fate answer

While on this date face to face

A Heartfelt Sum Warms Up Us

EPISODE 5

✦

QUESTIONS UPFRONT

When, both of us occupy, the same room space

Cautiously, censored words are spoken

Wherefore, you can have ongoing relations with companions

Really, every moment is enough, can you realize?

While, just to be quickly recognized

As' senior citizen is a worthwhile honor!

"although you foresaw close up"

Clearly, I wasn't a recall of your tainted former life

Questions Upfront

Foremost, at range, I confronted all false memories

"about us vividly seen in our room"

Madly, you became informed upfront,

And faced with your awful conduct

While, twenty four seven is versatile

Falsely, in fake affections to satisfy

Fore, somebody's misled thoughts for a roommate

Sadly, becomes an unsuccessful attempt

Questions Upfront

Selfishly, doesn't think about consequences

Playfully, taking part in a roll

And showing room mate bitter disgust

While, humbugging remarks leave seniors disturbed

Wherefore, roommate pretends to have known years of friendship

Solely, having to share a room with me is at fault

Fore, absurd are words coming out, the mouth of roommate

As' I don't have a hint to rooming with foolish behavior

Questions Upfront

You may be alone for mishaps,

And without a memory recap

Truly, I don't need to be part of a memory

Apparently, did not happen

Questions Upfront

EPISODE 6

A PERSONA OF INTRIGUE

I noticed a persona of intrigue,

And persona's brilliance has stunned

"my unending admiration for known persona"

Oddly, hover's over me with captivated followers

While, my ability to answer reoccurs

Wherefore, our motive to tag along with a persona of Intrigue

"good or bad is more than fascinating to behold!"

Yes, a glance at persona's own fashion style is curious!

Cheers From Friends To Celebrity

A impulse rushing unchecked

Aimlessly outward, off course

Socially, intrigue was the cause to charm more admirers

"swept into Persona's life, imitating life of known persona's title"

While, no matter how costly, without rechecking our steps

Energetically, mirrors pace walking in persona's footsteps!

"indeed a lifetime's given chase"

Yes, ceaseless stars of cheerfulness seen on show stage

Cheers From Friends To Celebrity

Why myself with followers' behavior?

Passionately never faded from us,

And seems to be a basis rarely explained

"about persona's effort for success"

As' ideal roll model luring fans

Highly, achieves ratings on numbers rising!

While, time to time, every second on minutes

Noticeable, capturing worldwide media
at any time or any place

Cheers From Friends To Celebrity

Clearly, a persona of intrigue is desirable

Fore, societies number of friends

A persona of intrigue has made

Gradually after some decades

Cheers From Friends To Celebrity

EPISODE 7

VACATION PLAN
NEEDS VARIABLES

Timely, my vacation is scheduled

Hurriedly, without wasting a moment's needs

Wherefore, accessible credentials packed inside of baggage

As' always avoiding repacking again

Carelessly, my essentials to note!

"after a while arrange transport"

Fore, car rental payment

And reliable on-hand funds

Beforehand travel assets

Unacceptable, provisions forgotten inside my baggage

"i may need to replace it with a manageable commodity"

Quickly before, I am confirmed on my boarding pass

While, allowing travel attendant to validate me

Passable, on-board travel access

Importantly, realized essentials with shoulder case

And fitted across chest to shoulder with a belt strap

Firmly, fastened to my personal wear is a good idea

Beforehand travel assets

Supposedly, if fault was a reason for missed departure, at my disposal alternative travel ticket

"trip schedule should have been planned"

Fore, my vacation receipt to pass

Therefore, would have to be modified

While, replacing other printed vacation receipts,

And recall another transporter to arrive at off-boarding station

Calmly, reaching the other side of gate

"travel will vary on itinerary"

Beforehand travel assets

Helpfully, soothing to notice traveling

Arriving on time at off-boarding station

Fore, on time as planned

As' always to meet my scheduled destination

Beforehand travel assets

EPISODE 8

⤫

LOOKOUT SEARCHES
OUT IN THE DISTANCE

Sir Milton Sr. knows keeping his head above clouds
is worthwhile

"since the site of rainy storms is nowhere!"

Calmly, staying away from turbulence

Usually, steering through a safe course

Sir Milton Sr. every second keeps his bearing

"although, confident marine challenges is child's
play"

While, seen without mistakes, he is favored

Doubly, steadfast to completing his tour

Lookout Searches Out In The Distance

Sir Milton Sr. Is experienced to stand

Honorably, at the helm countless times

While, aided by a compass to calculate

Fore, range north south west east,

And directions, a normal plight

Sir Milton Sr. checks routinely

"although, visibility may be blurred"

Suddenly, from a decline in air pressure

Lookout Searches Out In The Distance

A clear scope is visible of marine, he sees miles ahead, far off coastal shores

And changes coordinates without a seconds delay

Fore wasting no time sir milton sr. values time to rescue!

Whosoever, came to a unexpected demise

Foolishly disoriented, fallen overboard

"alerts safeguards to respond saving people, whom fell into water"

Hurriedly acting, jumping into terrifying marine waters

Courageously, with lifesavers rescuing overboard victims

Lookout Searches Out In The Distance

While, threatened by uncanny high winds started unusual high tidal waves

Duly, well prepared for any unexpected weather,

And command station with doppler sensors for safety

Seasonally, sir milton sr.continuously sails to make another round of tours

Lookout Searches Out In The Distance

EPISODE 9

WHY THE TOSS
AROUND ON BOAT

Yes, notification awaits to hoist anchor

"sailing at ease parting land"

As' water currents carry a floating castle out to sea

Yes, a normal bon voyage, afloat boat cruise

As' any splendid sunny day in soothing heat on a boat's deck

"watching as I drift, drifting away slowly!"

While further outward, further passing beach shores

And watching the coast disappear from view

Why The Toss Around On Boat

I wonder why onboard accommodating?

Fore, schedule routines for cabin attendant

While, providing room service during a cruise

"noting a passenger using a stateroom"

Normally, boat cruise owner supply passenger needs

Timely, with fresh linen bath shower bed

While, using the stateroom's living space

Surely, pleasing boat owner's onboard passengers

Why The Toss Around On Boat

A plain routine could have been courtesy commanding

Fore, cabin attendant to give passenger leeway on boat owner's behalf

Leisurely, at my disposal all about boat to pass

Mostly than being placed on a premises

"aided by busy cabin attendants"

While, another cabin attendant help

Busily, comforts other passengers out of generosity,

And were anxiously awaiting help

Why The Toss Around On Boat

Don't bother cabin boys for comfort, they have another duty

Only, to serve boat crew on cruise is allowed

"how mind bothersome a boat cruise can become"

Fore, just to accommodate a passenger upfront

As' passenger assumes when purchasing a reservation with cruise boat

Occasionally, there was no effort!,

And Why Oh' Why accommodating passenger only applies only to the stateroom?

Evidently reserved for onboard passengers

Why The Toss Around On Boat

Welcoming passengers with jolly cheers

While, feelings after paying travel agent

Fore, stepping on cruise boat's deck is awestruck,

And boat captain's favorite notice said aloud is all aboard

Why The Toss Around On Boat

EPISODE 10

PANDEMONIUM ALERT

I am offensive against pandemics day and night.

"about viruses causing symptoms worldwide"

Sadly, on a articulate name is not impressive

"aka novel coronavirus covid-19 surfaced"

While, upsets of deaths were not relevant to recall!

Fore, covid-19, in introducing a cure how awful

Detestable, plague rudely scares us through social media,

And fearsome intro's of variants

Pandemonium Alert

News announcement intro of variants

Mysteriously, makes contaminant appear to be some kind of riddle to solve

Noticeably, clever, fabled, harmful creature

Fore, I am already on a offensive

Daily, against covid-19, from listening to news alerts,

And fear inspiring to corrupt, frightful virus covid-19 caused casualties

While, unconfined within the same time space at bodily range"

Fore, virus caused humankind to suffer

Pandemonium Alert

I am already on a offensive

While, unvaccinated humans ignore pandemic warning

Mainly, lowering health standards tempting a deathbed

Publicly, I fight to avert covid-19 public impact

Really, should be erased on televised news ratings.

Widely, a majority of people are living in pandemonium

Insanely, about disgusting appearance of viruses,

And numeric numbers in the teens added to alias name

Pandemonium Alert

Noisy old statements sounds unpleasant in society

While, trying to lure more people into your claws, trying is useless for Covid-19

Weekly no matter, a loud roar in this decade

I am on the offensive against Covid-19

Pandemonium Alert

EPISODE 11

⌒∞⌒

DAILY USES FOR A
RESIDENTIAL ROOM

Daily, I use a room of residence, this wasn't immediate

Idly, whenI leased room space,

And premises needed modification

Clearly, a impressive suitable place for others

While, including myself to convey your acceptance

Solely, I am able to have different sorts of festivity

Likely, a retreat for meditation!

Fore, inviting any number of guesses

At My Spacious Convenience

My residential room allows associates to have conversations

Fore, sharing subjects and arrange reunions

As' every day dated on occasion with a variety of functions,

And availability for anyone knowing a day will come

Desperately, looking everywhere,
unable to find room for rent

While, during hours nearing sunset, a glimpse of hope

Surprisingly, awaiting no longer, your face swells into a smile

Continuously, hearing a phone ring to invest in a room

At My Spacious Convenience

A valuable asset is my fortress of solitude

Humanely, using at my own discretion

Foremost, a organized freshly scented bathroom,

And shower extras to my room with occupants even vacant

Lately, automatic utensils for comfortable living

Spaciously, built-in folding table inside wall for all dining hours

Only, alarm sensors my room has capable to alert

Essentially, workers of unsafe conditions inside room

At My Spacious Convenience

I have control to make accessible,

And inaccessible to a room

While, leasing spacious residence

Fore, delighted living my life using a residential room

At My Spacious Convenience.

EPISODE 12

PUBLIC BILLBOARD
SHARES A STORY

My eyes were transfixed on a billboard

Vividly, conveying a story with a sandy sky-colored background,

And illustrations of colored exotic flora

Closely, plenty of large palms trees

Fore, ferns noticeable has made me inseparable

Simply, solving a artistic drawing's message in a tropical zone

While, eyesight dazzled with awe of unknown artist

"began to open my imagination"

Artistry Hypnotizing To Recall

Although, awesome in size, billboard can be seen

Fore, miles away, I saw a round enclosure,

And attached on top a square green leafy roof

Undeniably, viewed by the entire public on billboard

Brilliantly, displaying, author's handiwork to create

"depth-defying rainbow colors blended with images"

As' cotton candy cloud shapes,

And public couldn't help saying this is a time I won't forget

Artistry Hypnotizing To Recall

Near the bottom, a sand-colored background

"shows completed paint drawing of sandstone-colored mosaic"

Highly seen at center, a image painted of someone

Clearly, wearing a gown girded from the waist down,

And holding a water pouch on mosaic painting

While taking note, myself with everyone else at this minute

Socially, sharing media photo images with cellular phones

As' comments, images of billboard were sent back to our cellular phones

Artistry Hypnotizing To Recall

Everyone knew the billboard image they shared

Curiously, shows a story of mirage,

And oasis, about thirsty character

Early midday when first viewed by the public

Artistry Hypnotizing To Recall

EPISODE 13

∾⧓∾

HOW PRACTICAL FOOTWEAR IS TO THE OWNER

Oh, how practical footwear, I put on my feet

Healthy, safeness is a need for naked feet,

And all this time, I have made wearing footwear my endeavor

Fore, there is no choice from start to finish

I understand practical footwear wakes a owner up to fulfilling their attire

"presentable to oneself, as well other's wellbeing"

While, fitted for relief from stepping on hard ground surfaces

Happily, mindful always for healthy feet in any location

A Well Deserved Comfortable Feet Support

Oh, how the confines of practical footwear has made my feet feel alright

Dually, secure to a range without worrisome bother

Essentially brought to the attention of owner

While, owner may be adult, teenager

Overly, neither forgetting overactive juveniles, making this custom almost ceremonial

Oh, how factual ah, how valuable!

"parents caring for a infant buying baby socks"

Practically, safe footwear for a child's health

A Well Deserved Comfortable Feet Support

Wherefore, customizing active footwear size

Fore, adapting until feet feel relaxed,

And teaching how to keep balance

Daily, for whatever surrounding condition exists

While, every day practice, learning to wear footwear

"oh how practical is footwear"

Actively, never fails me in cold climates

Solely, freezing snow covered alps, tropical island beaches

A Well Deserved Comfortable Feet Support

I never disregard my practical footwear

As' just another clothing accessory

"Fore made dearly valuable"

I enjoy how practical footwear looks

While, size is adjustable for my feet

Purposely, mirrors respect to others,

And in return, I am able to share

"my effort into being manageable"

A Well Deserved Comfortable Feet Support

My practical footwear unfailing

Surely, always is with me,

And all terrains in any weather

Reliable from beginning to end

A Well Deserved Comfortable Feet Support

EPISODE 14

❧

SUNRISE TO SUNSET
STIMULATES ME

I enjoy sun rays shimmering through my window curtains

As' I wake up feeling rays of warm comfort on my face, a continuous feeling motivating me

As' I attend to my morning activities in washroom bedroom

And kitchen makes me ready to give godly thanks for waking up

Normally, seven days a week every morning

Early, having a meal at this time

Freshly, cleansed with a organized table

"noting I am heartily filled at breakfast!"

Sunrise To Sunset

Afterwards, sun rays in mid-afternoon

Brightly, shines upon a place I am at rest

"widening my eyes to open surroundings"

As' I participated in hourly time periods

"forthcoming newly felt wonderment again"

Fully, soothed me throughout hours, enlivened my body,

And soul to emerge in a very pleasant condition

Slowly, floating at daytime until my participation expires sun sets

Sunrise To Sunset

Myself with others are content with stimulation

While, watching spectacular unavoidable site

Fore, awhile longer, then warmth becomes faint,

And the sunlight dims today

Normally, this late afternoon, a recurring message

"well-known numbers of hours we shared together"

Freely, Clarifying the daily presence of the sun helping to comfort everyone

Purposely, changing many lives for another better day

Sunrise To Sunset

Sunny weekdays for several months

Fore, feeling lasting joy beyond sunset,

And resulting in not just another normal day

A typical sunrise to sunset day

Sunrise To Sunset

EPISODE 15

∘⤨∘

SIGNIFICANT DECISION
TO RECEIVE WINGS

My decision was timely for acceptance to reserve,
a west-wing penthouse apartment

Nicely, greeted inside the condominium's hotel, I
had to wait

While, entering a lounge area with accepted clients

"still completing their condominium paperwork"

Politely, clerk offered several bonuses

Foremost, dining breakfast steam bath,

And directions to boardwalk near ocean

While, viewing the scenery, I couldn't avoid noticing

Wings A Significant Change

Vacation tourists are inside condominium to buy a penthouse

"moving forward receptionist finished a transaction with me"

Graciously, some time has passed

Finally, next a decision for accommodation

While, given a directory showing quad room green room,

And penthouse rooms are the fanciest inside condominium

Openly, overlooking boardwalk from the north side penthouse room

Fantastically, surreal a aqua emerald colored ocean

Wings A Significant Change

Receptionists show courtesy sharing flier info

About, vacancies to bustling tourists with limited time offer

Luckily, west wing penthouse apartment reserved for me

Initially, confirmed dates on my calendar's holidays

And accounted in helping schedule a timely reservation

While, Overwhelming to mention, validating my title for a plan to secure premises

"turnover to me west wing penthouse condominium bi-monthly, fits budget next to note of charge"

Finally, closure was done then said, <u>made</u> me glad to receive privileges

Wings A Significant Change

A place of simplicity complimented for being hospitable

Fore, paying attention inside penthouse west wing apartment

Widely, in motion helping yourself around, admiring how well ordered transparent display cases are kept,

And inside decorated winged medal awards with stripes

Clearly, viewing favorite accomplishments besides guess requests to browse

"I feel proud, especially when sun shines through windows easily"

While, encompassing the whole west wing at center display case, seen like sparkling gems

Brilliantly dazzling, as if this was my first time capturing this moment

Wings A Significant Change

Memorable goals accumulated settled

Timely, relieved my gold quest,

And rekindled comforting moments with swift streams

Softly, winds of warm embrace

Wings A Significant Change

EPISODE 16

RELENTLESS NATURE

Relentless nature constantly flows to share your outlook

While, living in a populated world body and soul

Cautiously, taking whatever passes your way at any moment,

And your presence will unfold sensations unfelt

"now these very countless minutes"

While, a couple of minutes later

Fore, sensations will be completely known to you

"today slightly fore every forthcoming day"

A Nature To Be Cautious About

Feeling pleasure displeasure leisure is ongoing every day

Naturally, experienced wherever life's cycle may be at ease

While, more than compassion to feeling love normally

As' if helplessly pulled into a sincere moment

Fore, a intangible emotion is already on the way

Freely, to your mind to communicate with someone else's mind

Therefore, thinking to decide whom is to judge my own acts

Only, Almighty God can release a confused mind

A Nature To Be Cautious About

Relentless is the mind's ability to be unconfined

As' having no bars being endless, making vital choices

About, where should you start, or where should you stop,

And if unclear given unto captivity without will power to act

As' requested confined reversed into a striving impulse to participate

Easily, guided by livelihood given permission for reliable help

Fore, benefiting a natural progress subduing marvelous wonders

While, support of oneself with multitude of others, anywhere a time of season interacts with lives

A Nature To Be Cautious About

A nature guide to safeness walkthrough

As' reliving safety lessons using trial by error

Fore, although relentless in bountiful nature

While, emerges sentience all around us

A Nature To Be Cautious About

EPISODE 17

❧

THE CHAPLAIN'S
PROGRESSION IS EVIDENT

Chaplain you came to aid our tent

unexpectedly, residents replied to chaplain, we are
in a distressed state

Monthly, our tents didn't expect someone versatile
in your status

Blindly, appeared from nowhere to reform our
tent's place

Personally, after noting tents humiliating condition

While, finding very unusual living conditions,

And low sanitary health standards

Chaplain a reverend, you are as noted imparting righteousness in various beliefs!

A Righteous Compromised Shared

Readily, to act, relieving depression surrounding our tent

Temporarily, in this space during assigned tour of duty,

And chaplain our lives confide in your ability to reveal our spirits

As' Progression in recovery, prolonging a state of social stability"

Clearly, living faithful to our community's prayers

"neither substituted with another religion!"

Chaplain duty demands, share your faith,

And protect those innocent, who can not fend for themselves

A Righteous Compromised Shared

Chaplain, wise you are to compare worshipping

Fore, many of our tents pursue hope, allowing reasonable testimony

Fairly, preached in different religious cultures,

And spiritual groups various languages, ensuring our understanding

Firstly, remains sanctified, although, our holy beliefs have been misunderstood before

Lately, was our tents faith for having been mistaken

While, noticing chaplain set a path for everyone to understand

Surely, prayers were made for a better tomorrow secretly

A Righteous Compromised Shared

Confrontations with other cultural groups

Fore, emerged conflicts gave rise to holy wars,

And brought desolation that heretics caused

Quickly, there's no doubt our tents rely on the willingness of Chaplain

Daily, care for our standards at this time

While, our souls became unfit,

Overly, sensitive you are chaplain to revive our tents circle holy faith

Rightly, soul mission becomes his forthcoming tour of duty

A Righteous Compromised Shared

Chaplain a prayer to assure comfort is granted to suppress our feelings

Sadly, towards bitter deceased souls

Coldly, no longer alive in a world

Wherefore, climaxing became evident

A Righteous Compromised Shared

EPISODE 18

MEMORIES FOUNTAIN

Memory helps everybody in the reality of our existence,

And sharing real insight giving clarity to our values, creating glittering signals

Instantly that you're alive at this very second on a preeminent trek to retain thoughts

Smartly, reveals perceivable plans for upcoming relations

Lively, sparks on a path to clarify remembrance

"always ready to communicate until the appointed hour"

Plainly a mindscape already in sync

Fore, recalled to attend a special occasion

Complete Memory Outline

Noting lingering memories of past relations

Actually, moments formerly lived unveils a future,

And past lives in conjunction

"resembles a water fountain"

Closely, at the center of both future with past entwined together

While, flowing to refresh our encounters made

Slowly, at young age memorizing all your social contacts

Safely, storing to make useful when confronted in person

Complete Memory Outline

Memories from infancy to becoming older

Elderly, in age, someone will always recall days spent

Fore, living with a relative even though now a elder

A temporary loss of memorable times is wearisome

While, able to retain some memory to clarify needs

Forthcoming, has become a ability for survival

As' invisible memories to others whom remember

"searchable everywhere within your inner self"

Complete Memory Outline

Through emotional expressions, when a infant cries for attention,

And enlightens our memory purpose

While, leaving fence open to widen minds

Fore, exploring many more possibilities

Complete Memory Outline

EPISODE 19

WHY SO UNFORTUNATE

Hey, why so unfortunate!

Wherefore, I ask was there a reason

Recently, your implicit attitude made

Fore, all of a sudden calendar date

And perhaps circumstances begin to intimidate

Personally, welfare of immediate friends

"clarify where was you pushing going?"

Emotionally, after showing your very disturbed

A Unfortunate Case To Resolve

Under breath, you implied socially

Fore, waking up compassionate people

Closely, around trying to relate with you

Solely feeling, the same affection

Sincerely, towards value's unusual role

"explainable during calendar date noted today"

Hurriedly, to intervene being attentive to remarks

Mildly, impressions within the same recreational intersect

A Unfortunate Case To Resolve

While, inside same recreational space,

And friends readied to get involved

About, current status to resolve a report

Answerable, as to why so unfortunate

Carefully, noting fair reason needs to be answered for impressions

Highly, remarks unsettled to our conversation

Evidently, you will know drama

Gradually, will make you mindful

A Unfortunate Case To Resolve

Clearing clouded thoughts lingering

Numerously, around in the brain's cranium,

And counting each breath whispered

Fore what happened became apparent

A Unfortunate Case To Resolve

EPISODE 20

⌒∞⌒

MY RECOLLECTION
OF A BARGAIN

My recollections of a bargain

Wisely, made with anyone that's worthwhile

A trade for a requested valuable,

And I received ever so often

Notable, a bargain doesn't mean bargain wins

Fore, I recall, there was another bargain

Vividly, coming to mind my buddy's sister

Plainly, I said to her let's start dating for awhile

I Recollect A Bargain That Is Valuable

Firmly, standing by my word,

And what happened next was heard

A sound voice said to me from the babe

Oh' Yeah such manly stature, that's life forever!

While heard from my voice was yeah, right on time
music to my ears

Yeah, people may say oh that's nothing at all

Gladly, I said to her ownership of all bargains, like
commodities made me a score,

And happy rather than take a fall

I Recollect A Bargain That Is Valuable

Empires ruled in harmony,

And were neighborly during centuries

As' allies turning some into a adversary

Falsely, in front of empire's doorsteps

Fore, suddenly fell to pretenders

"a close up look at a empire that didn't choose friends carefully"

Stupidly, rather chose to lose security

While, outcome of this recollection was a story pulled out of the past

I Recollect A Bargain That Is Valuable

Yearning to rise pass bargain gambits

Currently, are my lines every time said to attend a bargain"

While, ever moving easily forward,

And there could be a bargaining deal

Mostly, using a full deck of cards

Beneficially to acquire a valuable commodity

While, deal to swap always doesn't mean bargainer is going to succeed in winning

Therefore, I would make in-depth offer, tipping balancing scales in my favor

I Recollect A Bargain That Is Valuable

Eagerly, awaiting a gold streak

And notifies me more than anything else

Only, counting a millstone to trade

Fairly, passing through the doors of success

I Recollect A Bargain That Is Valuable

EPISODE 21

❦

LIVE LIQUID SENSE AT CHILDHOOD TO ADULTHOOD

A child unbound youth wanders hometown early

"roaming with godspeed around familiar places"

As' several years passed becoming a lively known figure

Gradually solving how oneself mind grows

Plainly, making a gesture, this neighborhood playground,

And elementary school near me is mine for some years

Fore, partaking as being socially identifiable to this generation "visible to all in neighboring areas, whom especially need to identify with youths"

Child To Adult Liquid Sense

Census evaluates a reservoir of children immersed in a liquid pool

Fore, later childhood years passed by happily

Forthcoming, a change inherited to experience plenty of senses

As' life's course stimulates a child's bio bodily genes,

And spiritual growth during playful moments at school

While, following a hereditary guide free to absorb education

"provisions given by a responsible adult through childhood years"

Slowly, disappeared after a span of time

Child To Adult Liquid Sense

Adulthood suddenly arrived, impressions with remarks was tolerable,

And to mention how sensitivity has encircled adolescent years

Slowly becoming terminal leaving child of yesteryear behind

Early, years of infancy faraway mirror reflects image of adulthood

Fore, prolonged future already in motion

Clearly shows lifespan's range at a fine age

As' adult, riches were made renown to time's longevity

While, Forms adult's courage closely kept values in pace"

Child To Adult Liquid Sense

A primary necessity in reality

Purposely, gives common thoughts

Safely, guided adolescence livelihood,

And smartly ensured in this lifetime

Child To Adult Liquid Sense

EPISODE 22

❧

DOCTOR LATELY A AILMENT HAS DIMINISHED PATIENT'S VIGOR

Doctor doctor always straightforward to respond with patients

As' usual at any time or any place

Locally, licensed to use medical instruments,

And receive health history information

Primarily performing doctor roles every time

While, answering complaints in hospitals

Fore, every minute of the day, responsive to prescribe a antidote

Medically, giving suppressant to bothersome ailment

Vigor Lately This Decade Doctor

Revealed about patient's diagnosis

Fore, every time doctor, attentive to patients current status

As' they rely on your practice doctor to recommend a recovery method

Lately, Describing health lately acting, upon without wasting a moments notice,

And fitness advice for active daily routines

"helping patients recover their vigors image!"

While, expressions of despair on applicant forms gives details

Closely, examined by doctor's patient report of failing vigor

Vigor Lately This Decade Doctor

Fore, widespread recently admitted sufferers
having severe symptoms

A ailment doctor proposed confidently

A already prepared solution,

And noting helpful doctors help patients are able
to uplift their vigors image

Overly protective about keeping patient's fitness

Globally, medical health standards in this decade
of pandemonium

Barely unveiling widespread ailments worldwide

Certainly, patients immediate concern is to make
a time schedule for check-up

Vigor Lately This Decade Doctor

Virtual patients appointments visits

And in – patient office visits

Carefully, avoiding being a victim

While, in this health safety decade

Vigor Lately This Decade Doctor

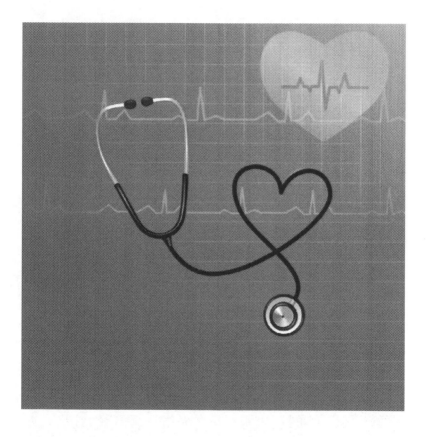

EPISODE 23

⸎

SHOW BIZ BABE AT CLUB (FEAT.) LYRICAL RAP VIBES

Babe you make business galore at the club

While, making a entry attracting faces of all bosses,

And fans beside gangster boys gangster girls surrounding show stage

"shiny stage lights following every footstep"

Daily, has everybody willing to pay for more explicit moves

Babe, as your fans are uncontrollable, listening to their own delight

Socially, keeping in rhythm with your lyrical rap gaining other fans attention

While, inside club showing off their crip gangsters dance'

Show Biz Vibes

Entertaining over exciting watching spectacular performance

While nicknaming you (aka) show biz babe,

And experienced in your stylish showbiz talents

As' fans are getting high quality one after another performance

"on stage grind babe popularity alias known as showbiz babe"

Readily, fine to perform a pole dance, displaying babes exquisite skin tight bathing suit outfit

Exotically, revealing her fine body dancing to the DJ's vibrant sounds

While, in pace with every movement made like a gymnast

Show Biz Vibes

As' vibes surround stage babe your in control of your steady balance

Easily you prance to make an outstanding elevated 360 degree circular motion on pole

Consistently, free sliding downward dancing prancing again using pole dance

Lightly, making a famous off stage exit, babe performs to DJ's sounds with drum bass beat

As' you balance upward pole dance performing 160 degrees, flexing bare long slim legs bouncing'

And spinning in a downside position free sliding down sideways gently

While, pushing away smoothly off pole dance, collecting cash money

Yes' fans, gangsters with bosses were expressing feelings"

Show Biz Vibes

Fore, showbiz babe time pole dancing,

And stay awhile longer in fan's view

Steadily, throwing money on show stage

While, showbiz babe skips off stage

Show Biz Vibes

EPISODE 24

WEATHER MAP 360
SENSITIVE REACTION

Weather ahead is now behind

Fore, I just don't mean behind

Really, I mean always feeling climate affects

Coldly, around from a range unbearable

Fore, I couldn't rest now continuing on my way

While, noting to view weather's pressure

"feeling weathers inescapable embrace"

And there's no range far enough

Physically, there's no range far enough, I can go to lose weather's affect

360 Degree Reaction

On my body and soul 360 degrees there is no refuge

I can reach quickly reach enough from weather above my head

Therefore, unprotected from harsh elements at my location

Fore, weather map informs weather's affect is close right under my feet

Evidently, penetrating foundation where I stand,

And finally weather's limitless energy takes hold on my body and soul

While, quickly awoken from weather's undefined pressure

Bitterly released upon my body and soul all around to no avail

360 Degree Reaction

I am already exposed with nowhere to escape

Therefore, tremendous howling winds warns me to close my window

As' pouring rain without suspension soaked landscape

"timely seasonal cycle with a heat wave following my innovativeness"

As' chilling is icy snow tempted me to find warmth

Safely, weather storms I hope to never encounter,

And a few others on weather map coming to nearly experience

"locally viewed by name as weather changes in climate"

360 Degree Reaction

Fore, my sensitivity is more responsive to my venture, immediately affecting my body's soul

Smartly, giving me a choice to be aware of resources

And freely subdue nature's surrounding area to help ease or halt the weathers impact

Progressively, on me and other's creating a barrier

Firstly, a shelter for sturdy weather protection

While making a responsibility, being resistant to weathers 360 degrees reaction

"nearby presence within range of my human senses!"

Fore, conditions being no longer subtable to live

360 Degree Reaction

Mostly, weathers affect on health,

And causes local catastrophes

While, volunteers recover residents homeland

Fore, relentless atmospheric pressure differential to my sensitivity

360 degree reaction

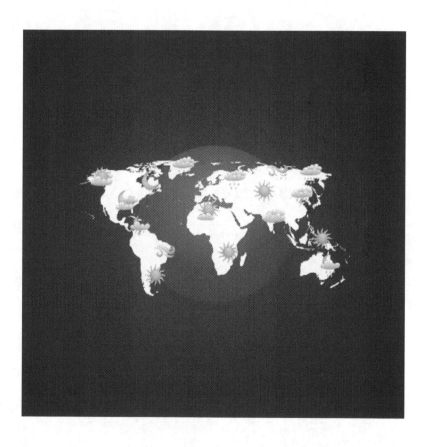

EPISODE 25

⸎

QUICKLY PASSING THE
HOUR ALREADY PLANNED

Already planned without rechecking one hour

Swiftly, lapses away onto another recurring hour

Logically, designed for any kind of program social
relevance

Fore, clockwork one hour readily prepared again
time again

Hourly, will pass away quickly recalling a past
occurrence

"noting in sequence elapsed hours viewed by
numbers"

Therefore, giving notification to standard time zones

And reports hourly shifts during a day

An Hour Already Planned

A normalcy for a timepiece to rate a timeframe completed

As' well a valuable device to have for passing hours

Readily, planned in sequence quickly passing hours

Fore' already planned gives notification about hour,

And date when holidays begins and ends

Therefore, keeping information well in mind

"today for holiday hour's yearly start date"

While, keeping important plans around the clock

An Hour Already Planned

Manually, planned news advisory quickly reports

"details on current conditions in town or state"

As' passing hours on land becomes short'

And announces alternative health wise method

"safely helping to announce timed alerts"

Firstly, gather together essential workers

"secondary notify families next hours ahead"

While, public transport vehicles is being sanitized

An Hour Already Planned

Fore, national emergency in effect

While, securing a defense line,

And deterrent plus safety measures

Verily, planned before one hour began

An Hour Already Planned

Printed in the United States
by Baker & Taylor Publisher Services